Fruits
from the
Poetry Planet

also by Ngozi Olivia Osuoha

The Transformation Train
Letter to My Unborn
Sensation
Tropical Escape (co-author)

Fruits from the Poetry Planet

by
Ngozi Olivia Osuoha

Poetic Justice Books & Arts
Port Saint Lucie, Florida

©2019 Ngozi Olivia Osuoha

book design and layout: SpiNDec, Port Saint Lucie, FL
cover image: *Welcome Home*, ©2018 Kris Haggblom

All rights reserved.

No part of this book may be used or reproduced in any manner whatsoever without written permission except in the case of brief quotations embodied in critical articles and reviews. Members of educational institutions and organizations wishing to photocopy any of the work for classroom use, or authors, artists and publishers who would like to obtain permission for any material in the work, should contact the publisher.

Published by Poetic Justice Books
Port Saint Lucie, Florida
United States of America
www.poeticjusticebooks.com

ISBN: 978-1-950433-070

FIRST EDITION
10 9 8 7 6 5 4 3 2 1

DEDICATION

This poetry book is dedicated to all the administrators and moderators of the Facebook Groups POETRY PLANET and PLANET FOR THE BUDDING POETS, and especially LOVELY GARCIA.

table of contents

Cradle	3
The Future	5
Happiness	6
Magic	7
Permission	8
Truth	9
Follow Me	10
White Horse	12
Beauty	13
Young	14
The Wonderboy	15
Rhapsody	16
Deceit	17
Tele-Rose	18
Covenant	19
Lucifer	20
Dethroned	21
Chaos	22
Mistake	24
Justice	25
I Am Sorry	26
I'm Gonna Catch You	27
Abundance	28
Simple	29
My Friend	31
The Pledge	32
The Builder	33
Tender Love	35
Mystery	36
Honey	38

Awesome Nature	39
Little Princess	40
Good News	41
Memories	42
Paradise	43
Bloom	44
Heavenly Bodies	45
Tales by Moonlight	47
November in Bambang	48
Centenary	49
Life After Death	51
I Am Your Puppet	52
Show Me Your Heart	53
Full Moon	54
Beyond Joke	55
My Heartbeat	57
My Shadow	59
Falling	60
Password	61
Storm	62
Home	63
Wonderland	64
Oblivion	65
Dare Devil	66
Angel Lucifer	67
Fantasy	68
This Journey of Mine	70
Golden Princess	72
Impossible	73

Mother and Child	74
I Am Fed Up	75
Blue Balloons	76
Inspiration	77
Rainbow	78
Thunder	79
Stepping Stone	80
Blurry	81
The Unknown Planet	82
My Hope	83
Prisoner	84
I Am a Hunter	86
Mirror	87
Forgive	88
The Library	89
Flames	90
Fear Not	91
Study	92
Kaleidoscale	94
Equal and Opposite	95
A Rhythm of World Without End	96
Closure	97
Ignite Your Passion	98
Fairy Tales	99
Peacekeeper	100
Home Again	101
Time and Life	102
Leisure	103

The Pendulum	104
Fortune	105
Misfortune	106
Boundless Love	107
Glassy Palace	108
Communicate	110
Communication	111
Reverie	112
Daydream	113
The Moon in My Heart	114
The Heart that Bears the Moon	115
My Boy	116
Christmas Is Here	118

Fruits from the Poetry Planet

Introduction

Fruits from the Poetry Planet is a compilation of all my award winning poems as well as other poems in the daily and weekly poetry enhancement challenges, photo, day, word, and theme inspirations in both the **POETRY PLANET** and **PLANET FOR THE BUDDING POETS** groups, excluding the winning poems featured in the Group's Quarterly Anthology.

Cradle

For the jungle,
Here is the hurdle
That I must cuddle
For life is a struggle
And I must not fumble.

Lo, one can stumble
And also tumble
But it a gamble
I must not leave in shamble.

Up, I go
Further, I do
Farther, I see
Yonder, I flee
Up, I look
There, I book
Future, I cook
Mission, I hook
Lo, I leap
Lo, I lead.

Beyond, I head
Within, I dread
Without, I spread
Tender, I crawl
Poor, I move
Focused and determined

Someday, somehow
Sometime, somewhere
Sooner or later
I shall sing aloud
Mission accomplished.

The Future

The unborn dream

Here lies my candle

Of a unknown mother,
Pregnant with a future
A future so unknown
Yet clearly written.

Hunger ravages me
And tears me apart,
Loneliness befriends me
And boredom mourns me
Here, I am, a child so thirsty.

Poor me, in a land forsaken
Hopeless and helpless
None ever cares about my pretty hair.

My pure eyes see death
And my innocent face drink tears
Tears of an unknown future.

Happiness

The world is hell
And nothing is normal,
Everything has gone crazy
And life has become lazy.

The more you look
The less you see
The more you pray
The deadlier becomes,
Stranger things day by day
Ungodly roads wider and wider.

We wait to live
But actually we wait to die
Here, we are busy
But busy doing nothing
We yell and yell
We fail and fell,
But nothing really changes.

Happiness has eluded us
Anger is our sweetheart,
Our bed wails
Our pillow weeps
Happiness laughs at us.

The scorn rages
The scourge cages
Who sold our happiness
And question needing answers.

Magic

I am the magic
That binds you together
I run your head
And pump your blood,
I mingle with your soul
And tangle your hair,
I am the fingers
That caress and stroke you,
I am the magic that turns you on.

I am the stars
And the black magic

Permission

I am neither deaf nor dumb
I hear and speak
I say my mind,
My opinion is my might
I do not need your permission.

When I talk hear
When I hear talk
But your words are yours
And mine are mine.

Within my limit, I am bound
Within your limit, I am bound
Bound without, yet unbound
You have permission to read this.

I air my view
I listen to understand
However, permission granted.

Truth

My friend, Ruth
Has a painful tooth
So he cannot sooth
Even in her booth
And that is the truth

Follow Me

Sweetheart
Follow me to the temple
Come, let me show your love

Follow me to heaven
Let me teach you of joy
Let me abolish your sorrow.

Come honey
Follow me,
For life is only once.

Follow me
Let me take you to God
So that you can be with the angels.

Follow me
Forget this world,
Nothing befits you here.

Hold me
Hold my hand
Never let go
Do not look back
Just come along
See, the pathway
Enchanting and promising
Look, beauty beyond borders.

Follow me
I am your guide and guard
Your compass and map
Your must a pointer.

Follow me
Let's go there
Where peace and love abound.

White Horse

I am a white horse
I am strong and energetic
I am a stallion
I run marathon.

I am as beautiful as my environment
I am green at heart
And in blood too,
I am royal.

I care less about castles
I don't live in mansions,
I love heavens
But I wanna be here
Because I enjoy the terrain.

Forget those who lord me
I can do otherwise,
But for the sake of chariots
I am an angel.

This white horse you see
Is nothing but a god.

Beauty

Heavenly bodies
In blue light,
Full moon
In white
Rays of hope
Spreading all over the earth,
Dews of peace
Showers of blessing,
Glows of love
Giving calm a chance.

Young

I am young
And strong,
I am a song
I will do no wrong.

I am young
With a green tongue,
I am a gong
I sound loud.

I am young
I can bear Armstrong
I am young
Lively and vibrant
I will be vigilant
So that I become a giant.

The Wonderboy

Hey, you my lover
You are a wonder boy
You hold therein
And pet the ground.

You reach the sky
And somersault for me,
You wear me love
Instead of clothes.

Hey, you wonder boy
Impossible is nothing.

Rhapsody

You are a mystery
Like a wonder
I hardly comprehend.

You are supernatural
Difficult to decipher
Impossible to fathom,
Troubling to ascertain.

Jokes, tortures, turmoil
Chances, opportunities
Fears, lacks, uncertainties.

Enveloped in your beauty
Lost in your deceit.

Deceit

You are a green snake on a green grass
You hide to hurt and harm
You are the thunders that follow the lightning,
You hit in a twinkle.

You are the nightmare that ruins a sleep,
You come like a dream.

You are the tongue that twists truth
You lie to kill.

You are faceless
And coward that cannot love,
Your motives are destructive.

Tele-Rose

Do not send me a rose
If you are not mobile,
Give me no flowers
If you cannot see me,
For what use ornament
And what romance is in your call.

Miles severe
Distance separates,
Your voice and your rose
Can never love like you.

I do not want tele-rose
Be with me, forget roses
Stay here, I don't wanna call.

Covenant

I love covenants
I respect them,

I live covenants
I honour them.

I value covenants
I appreciate them,
I nurture covenants
I water them.

Your rings are beautiful
They are lovely,
They glitter and shine
They dazzle and sparkle
Would you be like them
Glittering and shining,
Dazzling and sparkling
Or you would be stinking
Like a whitened sepulcher.

Lucifer

Shy, disgraced and defined
Despite my beauty,
Little god I was
Holy and gorgeous
White and lovely
Clean and neat,
Yet mocked and abused.

Down with my gown
Torn in town,
Bitter and battered.

Dethroned

Shameful and remorseful
Cloned and abandoned
Tortured and fractured,
Stripped and whipped
Rotten and forgotten
Lonely and moody
Needless and useless
Shattered and scattered
Disgraced and dethroned.

Chaos

I am in trouble
How do I calm this
And have peace again,
How do I move on
From this cumbersome worry.

My head aches
My heart wars
My soul wanders
My spirit mourns
My mind skips
How do I have peace again.

Love is far away
Peace is totally gone
Trust is dead
Obedience is forgotten
Confidence is buried
Composure is shy
Maturity is stunt.

Lack, everywhere
Need, here and there
Want, piling
Courage, dwindling
Unity, evaporating.

Confusion and conflict
Chaos and rancor

Ripples and waves
Storms and fears,
How will peace reign again

Mistake

I thought you were a man
I never knew you were a beast,
I saw you as a human
Now I know you came to feast,
I felt you were real
Never knew you steal,
I believed I had found love
But you were a wild dove,
And dirty vulture
Without a culture,
You came to destroy
My life and joy

You sounded truthful
But you were woeful
You appeared godly
But you were unholy,
You looked trustworthy
But you were unhealthy
Your words were lies
And your aims were flies,
You were just a whitened sepulcher
But you told me you were an esquire,
And gold digger you were
And lured me everywhere,
You deceived me to fall for you
Loving you was a terrible mistake.

Justice

I am justice
I cannot be bribed,
I hold good and bad
I serve you what you deserve.

I am blind
For my eyes are closed,
I do not look at your face
I am a virgin
I have no lover,
So you cannot deceive me
With your love or lust.

The scale is blessing and curse
When you behave,
I bless
When you misbehave
I curse.

I am justice
I serve the right fingers
Choose for yourself how to behave.

Choose life and live
Choose death and die,
It is in your hands
I am here to serve you according.

I Am Sorry

I am sorry
It was not my fault,
I tried my best
It will never happen again.

Forgive and forget
It would be double tragedy
If I never told you.

I had no peace
My joy was stolen
And happiness gone
So I decided to pull the trigger
By telling you.

Please forgive
To err is human
And to forgive, divine.

I'm Gonna Catch You

I love you
I need you
We are meant to be
I know so.

Run, run as fast as you can
Run as far as you can
Run to wherever you want
Hide anywhere,
Lock up your heart
Chase everyone away,
I'm gonna catch you
For we belong together.

Abundance

O weep not
For I hear abundance,
Cry no more
For the rains shall come
And the land shall yield

There shall be plenty again
Dry your tears,
Calm thy breast
Look beyond the fears
For I hear of abundance.

Lo, the earth is fertile again
The harvest is bounteous
And the labourers are ready
Look, thy barns expand
And thy costs enlarge.

Weep no more for lack
Cry never again for starvation,
Abundance is here.

Blessed waters
Drink and be blessed,
Blessed lands
Till and gather
Blessed earth
Live and rejoice
For I hear abundance.

Simple

I will make my life simple
So that I don't run into costs
Costs that are unnecessary.

I would live between my income
So that I won't be a debtor,
Debtor beyond my purse.

I would befriend simple people
So that I don't get lured,
Lured above my policy.

Colours abound
They all, are beautiful
Colours abound,
They all, are wonderful.

If they seduce me
If they attract me
If they bewitch me
If they possess me,
Then, I would be gone

Life is great
But full of sweat
Life is green
But much unseen
Life is weird,
But also to the wild

Life is crazy
Especially to the lazy
Simplicity is a seed
Mostly, if your means are limited.

My Friend

I love you so dearly
I don't care if you are poor
I don't care if you are down
I love you just the way you are.

Hold me close
Hold on to me,
Hold me through
Hang in there,
I am here for you

No matter what happens
The ups and downs
The highs and lows
The smoothness and roughness
I will be with you.

You are just what I want
You understand my heartbeat
You know my feelings
And you quench them
You hide nothing
You play no games,
You are just you
I love you just like that.

The Pledge

I pledge to write
As long as I live
I pledge to inspire
As far as I can
I pledge to heal
As often as my might,
I pledge to tell
Nothing but the truth
I pledge to mankind
Not to deceive him
I pledge to humanity
To be honest and modest
But most importantly
I pledge to God, my maker
To serve Him with my talents.

The Builder

I am an architect
I design my house
I am a builder
I build my house.

This is my abode
I dwell here,
I rule this nest
And withstand every test.

I am the father
I head my family
I am a mother
I love my home.

Now I stand
I sow, I soar
I perch, I fly, I weather the storm
I work, I rest, I move on
I survive, I support, I strive.

I am beautiful
My home is green
Up here, I see hope
The future is bright.

Hard, it is through
But I never give up
Tedious, it is

But I have a dream,
Hectic and tasking
Demanding and challenging
But tomorrow is looking good.

Ahead, ahead
Forward ever, backward never
There is a light after the tunnel.

Tender Love

Sacred and innocent
Poor and meek,
Mild and green
Time and real,
Clean and neat
Beautiful and handsome
Wonderful and awesome
And pair so divine
Yet ignorant of life's realities
A gentle couple
Full of tender love.

Mystery

In her womb, I formed
After weeks and months,
I knew not the hour I was born.

Mysteriously, I grew
Day by you, very new
Bit by bit, I learned
Even till date, I still do.

The air I breathe
The hairs on my body
The organs in my body
My soul, my spirit
My mind, my brain
My nails and wounds
All these teach me mystery.

I sleep and wake up
Sometimes, I am terrified
Nightmares and dreams
Visions and revelations
Mysteries upon mysteries.

I am a nobody
But I hear stories,
I know nothing
But I see wonders,
Life is a mystery

The mystery of faith and life,
The mystery and death resurrection
The mystery of eternal life beliefs.

Myths, superstitions, histories
Proofs evidence, fate, coincidence
Science and technology
All these are mysteries.

Honey

Dear honey
You are sweeter than sugar
And thicker than water,
You are brown
And shiny like crown
You are dark
Hark, dear bee
Blessed be thy hive
And sting us not
For we always strive
To taste your honey
That tells how we love you.

Awesome Nature

Special, one of a kind
Unique, rarest of them
Calm, peaceful, green, lively
Young, promising, beautiful and serene
Restful cloud, blossoming grasses
And yellow roses
Purest of love
Cleanest of hands
Truest of hearts
Let me love you, this real
In a land of awesome nature.

Little Princess

Little princess
Gorgeous in your gown
Proud with your dock,
Both in matching colours
Navy, ash, cream and gold.

Little princess
Great with her pet
Oft and tender
Kind and caring
Friendly and welcoming.

Gorgeous princess
Greetings to the palace.

Good News

Greetings humble princess
I come in peace
The lord has sent me
To proclaim good news
I bring you love.

Cheer up, lowly damsel
I have come from heaven
To light your path
Here is freedom,
I bring you love.

I am your guardian angel
Do not be afraid.

Memories

Your memories live in us
How would I forget
The old times we had
And the lovely moments we shared,
The pure love you taught
And the real sacrifices you made,
The miracles you performed
And the wonders of old.

But who forgets
The ancient teachings under
The care of a grandma,
Mama, you were nothing
But a goddess,
Your memories live in us.

Paradise

Green and enchanting
With the purest of love,
Lively and booming
With the truest of peace,
Bright and calm
With the abundance of life,
The blossoms of calm
Joy, happiness and goodness,
And paradise without sorrow
Please take me there.

Bloom

And seasons differ so do times
And seeds vary, so do lands
Scatter thy seeds, wait for no man.

Lands are vast but a few farmers
Labourers are few, together with wages
But harvest is coming, so wait for no man.

Choose your seeds wisely
Till and fertilize your land,
Plant, weed, water
And watch it bloom
Then you will bountifully harvest.

Heavenly Bodies

Look up the sky
See the wonders of the creator,
Blue and white
Stars, moon and cloud.

Light, rays, beauty
Day, night, noon.

The rains, the fogs
The mist, the dews
The hail, the air
They are all beautiful.

Wonders unknown, mysteries unheard
The universe, the galaxies
The planets and orbits
Look, they all are wonderful.

You are different
I am different
But we live here
Under our creator.

The heavenly bodies are numerous
They are larger than we can imagine,
They make the earth awesome
And our world unique.

The eclipse, the revolution
The lightning, the thunder
The sun, and the atmosphere
Everything up there is a wonder.

Tales by Moonlight

I have been here all night
Waiting for family and friends,
Longing to hear your voices
But only the birds sing to me.

Whispers of boredom
And noises of loneliness,
Fears of strangeness
And excesses of need,
Yet I am still here waiting for
Tales by moonlight.

November in Bambang

Where are the budding poets
In the poetry planet,
Where are the stars
And the galaxies,
Where are the rays of the sun
And the light of the moon,
Where are these heavenly bodies
That strike the earth with
Beauty, beauty from the ink,
Come, let us merry together
This November in Bambang.

Centenary

A group of poets
From all over the world
A bunch of talents
In unity and one voice,
Spreading and integrating
Preaching and healing
With words and pictures.

Hundreds of them
Thousands of them
Beauty and flavour
Glorious and mysterious
Honey, stars, moonlight, voyages
Horses, pussy cats
Docks, little couples
Mistake, weaver bird
Beach boy, inking sand
Freedom, rhapsody
Simple, roses, abundance
Rings, phones, young, faceless
Happiness, permission, magic
Chaos, pledge
Pain, symbol of justice.

Different exercises
Daily poetry enchantment
Picture prompt exercise
Word and photo inspiration

Poetry for the budding poets,
And place of diverse gifts.

Happy centenary
Wishing you more celebrations.

Life After Death

Terrors everywhere, horrors in and out
War and religion, hunger and famine
Earthquakes and floods, tsunamis
Hurricanes and landslides, typhoons
Killings, ethnic cleansing, rituals
Hate, crimes, wildfires
Natural disasters, bigotry
Hopelessness and helplessness, fears and tears
Lord, I beseech thee to be in paradise eternally.

I Am Your Puppet

Hello beautiful
I bring you flower
Please take this rose
As a token of my love,
Do not say no
Instead make me your puppet
I will be near you always
Never to let go
Don't kill this love
From my master.

Show Me Your Heart

Show me your heart
Let me see how beautiful you are,
Show me not your face
Hide your silicon,
I don't wanna see those scars
Scars of surgeries
Surgeries for make up,
Hips, lips, breast, lashes, brows,
Whatever the surgeon added
Hide those ones from me
Show me your heart,
If it is pure, then you are beautiful.

Full Moon

An orange sky
Heralding sunset,
A mighty hawk
Spying against a foe,
A lovely morrow we hope.

Calm evening of a full moon
Soothing breeze of peace
Pleasurable night we rest,
Nature blows the trumpet
Dawn welcomes our freedom.

Beyond Joke

We do not understand them
Yes, all of them.

The comedians are terrible
They have gone crazy.

The politicians are busy
Busy, doing nothing.
I cannot understand their work
Their essence still baffles me.

The actors are funny
They go the extra mile,
Reality contradicts life.

The students are weird
Absurd and reluctant,
Education is gone
Academics is finished,
Learning is gone
Intellectuality, forgone.

See, our world is messed
The future is uncertain,
The unborn is afraid
Which way are we heading to

I am not joking
Neither is this a joke,

Beware of doom
There is a gloom
If noon stands still
And night breaks no dawn
Then, we all are beyond joke.

My Heartbeat

Written all over me
As I wear a gorgeous smile
My heart beats for you.

Written in and out
Beyond imagination
My heart searches for you.

My soul works around
My spirit yearns for you,
My mind says it loud
You are the one.

This love you send
Glitters all around me,
It shines my path
And rekindles my passion
I know you are just the one.

I smile, my heart gladdens
Yes, I know, I love you.

My heart yearns for reality
Now, reality is you.
My heart longs for peace
Now, peace is you,

Dazzling like diamond
My life dazzles,

Radiating the joy you bring
Nothing can hide this love,
It just glitters.

My Shadow

Looking deep down
I see a brother
He looks inquisitive
Wanting to touch me
To hug and cheer me
But he cannot
Despite how we try,
He is as worried as I am
And as calm as I am too,
We pant and move together
Everything in unison
O it was only my shadow.

Falling

This is Kilimanjaro
Higher than a tower
The highest mountain in Africa
But it cannot weigh me down
Because I am African.

This is Everest
The highest mountain in the world
It cannot weigh me down
Because I am not afraid,
I am a citizen, citizen of the world.

Their towers shall bring me showers
Their valleys shall bring me shelter
Their trees shall bring me shade,
Timber and house
I shall fear no fall.

Scary, weary and dreary
Scared, weak and tired
Lonely and bored
Hungry and thirsty
Likely to fall
But I am on the move.

Climbing, higher and higher
Getting better and better
Hoping stronger and stronger
I fear no fall.

Password

Password is a code
That you alone decode,
Never make it nude
No matter how crude,
Even if you are Jude
Be not that rude.

Password is a key
It has a padlock
If you allow a monkey
To place a rock,
Then the donkey
May not carry the block.

Password is a secret
Make it concrete
If it is not complete
You may lose the fight
Despite the light.

But when things go sour
At the dark hour,
You may give the password.

Storm

My boot upon a stormy blast
Racing towards a towering mast,
Hoping to forget this bloody past
But looking back to see a lifeless cast.

Fighting hard to quench an ugly scene
Holding on to have a lovely serene,
But from all I have heard and seen
I know not where I have not been.

Stormy past and troubled present
Troubled life and waving future
This storm is blowing hard.

Home

Grandma is dead
Grandpa is dead,
No one at home
And all gone
Scattered north, west, south
And east
Hustling to make ends meet.

Cobwebs, rats and lizards
Spirits, ghosts and animals
Dilapidated and abandoned home
We are going home for reunion.

Wonderland

Follow me to a trip
Come, let me show you wonderland.

Come and see beauty
In a cave of modern rock
Like a goldmine
That produces diamonds
Follow me to this wonderland.

Shiny like streets of heaven
Quiet like a graveyard
Dreary like a thick forest
Lonely like a desert
But beautiful and a calm abode.

Come and see wonders
Wonders beyond nature,
Rocky, archly and curvy
Strong and bold
A place of vacations.

Silence of questioning trip
Sightseeing of fearful travel
The abode of lonesome wonder.

Light of light, sacred
Shrine of unknown goddess
Pure and gracious
So frightening, a wonderland.

Oblivion

I am a stallion
Living in a pavilion
With a ton of scorpion
In communion
With the bandwagon,
The union
Is over a million
Yet dying in oblivion
Because the dragon
Can only vomit crayon.

Dare Devil

Up above the world so high
Right inside the moon
On the blue sky
Riding to heaven,
Journey of countless miles
Effort of numerous strength
Determined and committed
No holding back
Ahead, ahead, no turning back
Forever ever, up above the world so high
Like a daredevil.

Angel Lucifer

But you told me you loved me
That nothing would ever come between us,
You swore to make me happy
And help me reach my destination
You promised to fight me for me
And keep me protected,
How come you were a roaring lion
The wolf and the tiger,
The beast that was sent to eat my flesh,
So you were a green snake on a green grass,
The angel Lucifer and Lucifer the angel.

Fantasy

Wake up
Why do you dwell in fantasy
Wake up
And face reality
For lovers don't dance in heaven.

Diamonds are not in hell
Neither are gold there,
There are no silvers there
Nor rubies,
Don't you know that this earth is hell
And lovers don't last.

Wake up
The sky is blue
Yes, true
But the land isn't of glass but grass,
It is only diamonds that dazzle
Sands don't nor muds
Here, trees are green not red
If you see otherwise, run.

Wake up dear angel
Life is not a dancehall
Lands are full of mines
They know not dancing shoes
They go off at any slightest touch
Beware of dancers

Even when they dance away their sorrow.

Fantasies, infatuations and lust
They all dance too, sometimes even better.

This Journey of Mine

I have understood that I and none
Just one single me,
Created none and sent into the world
To do exploits.

In this journey of mine
I don't have to take any routes
Because I have and defined destination
Definite and pronounced,
Not all roads can lead me there.

If I take shortcuts
I may land in trouble,
If I take wrong lanes
I would miss my track,
If I follow the crowd
I would be totally lost,
If I join the bandwagon
I would be lie them,
If I go their path
I would lose my home.

This journey of mine
Is unique, specific and outstanding
I need to be focused and exact
Lest the roadside distractions lure me away.

Chosen for a goal
Called for a purpose

Ordained for a mission,
Anointed for a curse
Commissioned and sent
I need not lose my vision.

So frustrating and cruel a life
So ungodly and inhumane a world,
Lord, I need thy grace
To arrive at my destination.

Golden Princess

Golden princess
How are you
Are you tending to your golden goose.

Little princess
Shepherd by the sea
Are you feeding your flock
And quenching their thirst.

Beautiful angel
The caregiver and lover of her flock,
I wish you peace and safety.

Impossible

Dear friend
I hope you are fine
I write to tell you my ordeal
I have been divorced long ago,
My wife was sacked from her job
Because she had HIV and cancer,
I am confiding in you, please
Don't tell anyone.
It hasn't been easy since then,
In fact life seemed impossible.

Mother and Child

Reddish cheeks worn out in sorrow
Weak legs torn by trekking
Pale bodies looking trashy
Hungry mother and child
Wallowing in forest.

Lost, seeking a way out
Wandering further and farther
Homeless, hopeless and cheerless
Mother and child, abandoned.

Smile on me dear fate
I look toward thy home call
From this untoward movement.

I Am Fed Up

How many more tens would I rape
How many more hundreds would I shoot,
How many more thousands would I kill
How many more millions would I bomb,
How many more would I displace before I die.

Tell me, tell me, O tell me
How many more would I kill
I smell blood, I drink blood
I wear blood, I sleep blood,
I see blood, I eat blood,
Everything, everywhere is blood.

I am fed up, I am no more a human
My family is lonely, waiting and praying for me
But here am I, killing and wasting others.

What is life if it should be wasted?
What is love if it should be lonely?
What is human if humanity is at war?
What is leadership if it is a tug of war?

I see shadows and spirits
Ghosts haunt and torment me,
Voices chase me up and down,
I have no peace, my conscience is dead
I am no longer human
I detest this life, I don't wanna kill no more.

Blue Balloons

Blue balloons
Powerful parachute
Take me up the sky
Fly me round the world,
Let me see the universe
And the wonders of creation.

Inspiration

Divine fountains of nourishment
Overwhelming wisdom of excellence
Peaceful pride of radiating love
Amazing touch of serenity.

Boundless force of love
Limitless power of anger,
Countless strides of fate
Choice-less gifts bestowed.

Inspirations of greatness
Shooting destinies like stars
Extravagant creator.

Rainbow

Darling you are my rainbow
You give me the colours of life
And the reasons to live,
You show me the depths of love
And the fears of living
You take me away to the heights of doubts
And lows of want,
You teach me the values of the universe
And the troubles thereof,
You represent each colour of the rainbow.

Thunder

Light, the fastest traveler
Moving along paths chosen
Striking whatever mysteries
Unraveling deep things of darkness.

Thunder, the noisy traveler
The voice of the heavens
Summoning ungodliness
Exposing filthiness.

Lightning, the quiet choker
And the silent killer
The announcer of thunder.

Ultraviolet rays penetrating incandescent objects
Radiations of high degrees
You are still a wonder to me.

Strike not the just
Spare the poor
Save the innocent
Safeguard the unloved.

Stepping Stone

I am not afraid of this sea
Nor the raging tempest,
I fear not the wave
Nor the troubling tide,
For these turbulence
Shall end in peaceful song.

Dark nights get me thinking
Its bunch of darkness grip me like a giant
But I fear them not
Because these stones shall be my ladder.

I have seen troubles and sorrows
I have known pain and anger
But they all shall sing my victory song.

Bondage and slavery
Be they temporal or permanent
They have their expiry dates
And they turn a stepping stone.

I shall not fall into this sea
Neither shall it swallow me up,
For these stones shall be my stepping stones.

Freedom is coming tomorrow
Lo, I am victorious.

Blurry

This blurry shadow of mine is shunting my view
Light rays and sunshine making it hard to see,
This life of black and white pages
Things so plain yet not crystal,
Issues discouraging and overwhelming
Who in their right senses cannot comprehend
Tell me life is a basket so woven beyond discernment.

The Unknown Planet

Seems like a new planet
One without form and void
Yet unnamed,
Brown, blue, green, grey and white
A sea like a muddy one.

Calm, quiet with no life
Strange like the land of the deep,
Who knows what the future holds here.

A hole of mysterious depth
An abyss, who knows.

Maybe a new planet
Maybe an old one,
Maybe a dead land
Maybe a dead sea
Who knows what fate.

My Hope

I am in the world
But I do not belong here
I am a stranger
Here for a purpose and with a reason,
I am a labourer
In the vineyard of my father.

Someday I would be gone
Gone for good.
I would return to my maker
To account for my mission.

My hope is eternal
I am not for physical and material pleasures
I am a human
But in and course, here on earth.

I look up to God the maker and creator
There, I focus
I hope solely on him
For ages past, on and to come.

On Christ alone, I build
My trust, hope, faith and future
In him alone, I wait.

Prisoner

For all the people wrongly accused
For all the people framed up,
For all the men set up
And all the ladies jailed innocently,
This poem is for you.

I write to remember you all
This may not reach you,
It may never liberate you
It may not seek and redress
It may never give you peace,
But I am just writing it for you all.

For all the souls who died in prison
And the ones in detention,
For those who are on death row
And those already executed,
For those who power, politics,
Religion and racism imprisoned,
This is for you all.

War might have done its worst
Terrorism might also have,
Hate, bribery and corruption as well
But none of you is forgotten.

Today, I write for your souls
Wherever you are,

Whatever made you prisoners
This ink petitions that cause.

Not forgotten, never forgotten
We are still here, on the course of humanity.

I Am a Hunter

I am a hunter
A wanderer and traveler
I am wandering everywhere
Traveling round and around the world,
Hunting war, violence, religion,
Abuse, rape, racism and hate,
Yes, I am a poetic hunter
My ink haunts and hunts all evil.

Mirror

I am a mirror
Mirror of world,
I reflect on things
For the world to reflect on,
My ink is a reflection
For the world to ponder
And meditate and repent.

Forgive

For your own good
You have to forgive,
Because bitterness is a hindrance
It kills happiness and joy.

Forgive, for your own peace
If you want to move on
So that you can love again
On a plain sheet
With a clean heart
And fresh mind.

Forgive, it is necessary
No matter the wrong,
The gravity and magnitude
Only then, you can cope.

Forgiveness is divine
It comes it's one to divinity
To err is human, to forgive.

Forgive yourself, no matter what
The errors, the mistakes, the regrets
The pains, let it go.
Life is a mystery
And we live by learning mysteries.

Bitterness is a burden, very cumbersome
It is a hedge that shunts blessings and breakthroughs,
Allow the angel of God to you totally.

The Library

Hello dear
I am John
Hi, I am Lizzy
John; nice to meet you
Lizzy; same here,
John; do you always come around the library
Lizzy; yes, I love reading, I write too
John; amazing, could we be friends
Lizzy; yes, as long and you read and write.

Flames

The gang knew their bang
So as they sang and rang
Men hid their bags in rags.

The game is same everywhere
But they blame the lame,
When they get name and fame.

The world therefore is in flames
Their fames are games,
So they tame and tame us
While they go up in flames.

Fear Not

Fear not, poor damsel
I feel your remorse
I understand your shame and regret,
It is written all over you,
Worry not
You have been forgiven and cleansed,
From today, you are no longer a sinner
Welcome home, child of God.

Study

Study, son, study
For only by studying, you can learn.

Learn, son, learn
For only by learning, you can read.

Read, son, read
For only by reading, you can grow.

Grow, son, grow
For only by growing, you can live.

Live, son, live
For only by living, you can know.

Know, son, know
For only by knowing, you can understand.

Understand, son, understand
For only by understanding, you can rule.

Rule, son, rule
For only by ruling, you can change the world.

Son, you must yearn to climb
For climbing shows you the other and deeper side of the world.

Your teachers are your ladder

Dead or alive, gone or around
Respect them, honour them
For without them, you may not go far.

Kaleidoscope

My glass prism
The reflection of my rays
My incident and reflected rays
The colours of my ultraviolet radiation
My gamma, beta and x-ray
You are my incandescent objects
You move with the speed of light.

You shine like diamonds
And glitter like gold
You dazzle like silver
And sparkle like ruby
You are more than a gem.

Your colours beautify me
No matter how I look at you,
I see beauty
Your reflections make me crazy
I reflect on you like a mirror.

You are like the sun too
Shiny, hot and illuminating
You are the light.

Warm, calm, lovely, loving
Lively and caring
You are my kaleidoscope,
A bunch of perfection for my reflection.

Equal and Opposite

We are not twins
Let not our make confuse you,
We are not husband and wife
But we are a couple,
White and spherical
We are rectangular
Sky blue and orange,
We have a man
In between us,
He acts and reacts with us
Because action and reaction,
Like Newton propounded,
Are equal and opposite.

A Rhythm of World Without End

Red, orange, yellow, green, blue, indigo, violet,
Like a waterfall it gushes,
Mesmerizing me with beauty
Fountains of peace and love.

River rainbow
Colouring my thirst
Seductive and attractive
O wonderful river
How beautiful you are.

Harmony of waves and storms
Energetic time and tide
Patches of nature and sleeping tempest,
Coastal powers from beyond
Ripples of a supernatural god.

Melodies voices of loud serene
Spirits of traditional joy
Echoes of freedom and true love
Harping on harps of unity
A rhythm of world without end.

A cluster of rivers in a galaxy of universe
Galaxy for oneness, living one.

Closure

Daily I thank God
I praise his name continually
For everything he created
And all he gave us,
But I thank him more
For Facebook, Twitter, Instagram and all social media
I imagine what the world would have been without them
The friends, name, breakthrough, connection and the wonders
We have made and learnt through them.
Hence, I cannot imagine their closure.

Ignite Your Passion

There is a dormant god in you
Waiting to be awakened,
He is a fighter and a winner
He can chase away demons,
Just wake him up
And watch him fight for you.

There is a sleeping giant in you
Starving, to be fed
To be quenched of thirst,
Feed him, water him
And watch him regenerate.

There is a hero in you
Your ignorance is dwarfing him,
There is a legend in you
Your dormancy is shunting him,
There is a guru in you
Your carelessness is killing him,
There is a superpower in you
Your lagging behind is burying him
Wake up, ignite your passion.

This world cannot be any better
This life cannot be any livelier
This hope cannot be any greener
Except you ignite that passion to make it beautiful.

Ignite, the world waits
Would she wait in vain?

Fairy Tales

Blue fantasies
Yellow butterflies
Fairy tales of captivating nature,
Amidst hilly tree
Full moon of pure illumination
Sharing sequence of silence
Great fixture of diversifying posture
Array of beauty in quiet orchestra.

Fairy tales o peaceful chaos
Telling visions of naughty story.

Peacekeeper

Today, off I go
Into the world beyond
North, south, east and west
All nooks and crannies
For blessed is he that makes peace.

I hate wars, wars are terrible
I hate terrors, terrors are horrible
I hate violence, violence is inhumane
I hate troubles, they all ungodly

With words, actions and prayers
With commitment, dedication and selfishness
I would seek peace and maintain it.

Enough pain and sorrow
Much hate and envy
Lo bitterness and jealousy
All these cannot give us peace

Peace is holy, friendly and cheerful
Accommodating, welcoming and appreciating.

I am a peacekeeper, I hope you are
Let us our brother's keepers
Only then can we live in peace.

Home Again

In the front line I am
Shooting and killing our foe
Defending our fatherland
Warding off preys and enemies
Retaining our grounds and territories
But so lonely and missing home
Wishing and wanting to be with you, the love of my life
O how desperately I need you, to see your face, those hopeful eyes
Home again, when shall I see my home, my native land
Never, will I forget you, dead or alive.

Time and Life

There is a time for everything
A time to be born and a time to die
A time to grow and a time to learn.

From birth to cradle
Cradle to toddler
Toddler to teen
Adolescence to adulthood
These phases and stages with their challenges

When nakedness is ignorance and childishness
When dressing up is necessity and dignity,
When carelessness is lack of interest and old age,
When old age finally gets to the grave.

The girl child is a treasure
Born and nurtured, she becomes a beauty queen
Married, she bears a child.

Works, and retires
Wears and ages
Becomes sick and dies.

Every phase of her life is not rosy
But she pretends and manages

Her legacy lives on
Long after she is gone,
The world never forgets her
No matter the power of the grave

Leisure

Playing with my granddaughter
To ease boredom
I see the excitement on her face
Spending quality time together,
Turn y turn, two of us
We take turns
After the play, we take a walk
After the walk we play the ludo
On and on, we chat
And I teach her mysteries and life,
O happy she is, curious and eager
Inquisitive and lively
Our couple is a blessing, grannies love a bunch

The Pendulum

Listen my grandchild
I brought you here to teach you a lesson
The lesson of life.

As I swing to and fro
Front and back
Up and down sideways on this pendulum
So would life swing you,
Not because of me you or anyone else
But because that is life.

Life swings us all no matter who you are,
Where you are or what you can achieve.
Never kill yourself during those swinging moments
Like I hold these chains just hold on to God
And he would reveal tremendous mysteries to you

Cruel, harsh, great, joyous, or however
Do not fail to remember this day,
The day I brought you here
Here, on this swinging pendulum.

Fortune

Warrior goddess
Send me happiness
Let it be gone, this loneliness
For troubles abound
Even with nothing found,
Please come quick with fortune
That my world be in tune.

Misfortune

Despite history
The future is a mystery
We have no control over it
Bit by bit, fit or unfit
We can only pray and hope
That we cross the tedious rope,
But in all, fall or call
We long to be tall,
We cherish fortunes
And wall against misfortunes.

Boundless Love

Even in the worlds beyond
My spirit still craves for you
I hug you with all my soul
And wish we never part,
I see a new world
Where we live as angels
Loving ourselves better
Holding on to our dreams
Never letting anything come between us
Because this chemistry is supernatural
A boundless love indebted to divinity.

Glassy Palace

Great place
Of colourful building
Dark, navy, white
Beautiful trees and fountain
Telling the age of kingdom.

Ages of judgment
Decades of injustice
Years of trouble
Centuries of pain,
Tales of humans
Stories of humanity.

Glassy, but not rosy
Shiny, but not modern
Dazzling, but not pure
Place of yesteryears.

Leaves of booming shade
Water of healing balm
The altar of solution
And the bed of war.

Royalty, respect
Honour, loyalty
Wisdom, integrity
Pride, ego
Power, leadership
Laws and order.

Glassy place of central fountain
Like a cathedral of mighty edifice
Old, knowledge and historical.

Communicate

Dear couples,
No matter the love
Communication is key.

Live life to the fullest
Enjoy it while it lasts
Dear friends
Open up
No holding back.

Forget your sorrows
Look up to God,
Hope and be glad
For tomorrow is a mystery.

Signs and symbols
Gestures and postures
All communicate.

Use whatever means
Reach your people
Life is once.

Communication

Mothers chat with their unborn
Fetuses talk to their mothers
It all starts from the womb.

Nothing is hidden
But something can be hidden
The world is vast
Make it closer.

Push, pray until something happens
Create ways to socialize
Live up to expectations,
Talking, loving, playing
All count.

Relationships thrive on communication
Even animals do too,
All living things communicate to survive.

Dreams, visions, revelations
Prophecies, incantations and the likes
All are messages for appropriate actions.

Reverie

Lost, in you
Hoping to be loved
Wishing you were mine
Prayed to have you
To be with you forever
But all was in vain.

You were more than a crush
Everything I wanted was in you
I could not imagine losing you
Losing you to a stranger
Someone who is not worth it.

But actually went wrong
Were you that cowardice?
That you could not choose
Or you were blind.

All day, fantasized about you
All night, I wished you were near me,
I believed you were just mine
O how I got it all wrong.

Daydream

Somebody wake me up
Wake me up from this deep sleep
This sleep is turning devilish
It is becoming barbaric
For all I am seeing is impossible.

You lived in me
Because I loved you,
So I believed you lived in me too,
How come I was only a fool?
Loving in an uncertain world.

Deep, I was gone, into you
Far, far away, I thought we were one
I told them we belonged together
I should have seen it coming

But all along, you knew
You knew we would never be
You hid it, and kept it away from me
So you pulled your shock absorber
Correctly and timely on guard
Fooling me, as I fooled myself
Thinking I was loving the real person
But you were the fake one, not me.

The Moon in My Heart

Look here, my love
I am lonely
Sitting by this cave
The cave of an onshore
Waiting patiently for you,
Do you see my heart?
It bears the moon
The full moon lives in my heart
It will give you light
Light for fairy tales
It will give you peace
Peace in a chaotic world
It will give you love
Love in a troubled earth
Come, love me dear.

The Heart that Bears the Moon

My heart houses the moon
Solely for you,
The moon lives in my heart
Just to make you happy

Look and live
Live, walk, and dwell in the light.

Bother no more of darkness
For within me is light,
In this shore of calm sail
I will give you love unbounded

The sea is calm
So is my love,
The shores are vast
So is my zeal
The tide is asleep
So is the tempest,
Come my love
For my heart belongs to you

Do not be fooled
Never be deceived
I bear the full moon
To disperse darkness and doom
Love me now and forever

My Boy

Go, my boy, go
Do it, you can
You are strong like daddy
Yes, you are strong.

Ride, ride, my son
You can tour the world
Do not be afraid
Ride, ride to glory
You have the power

Bravo, Hurray, Speed up
Speed up, son
I did exactly so at your age
I won, I won severally
And my own dad applauded me
Win son, so that I can applaud you.

Go, go, son go
Ride on, speed up
Never be afraid
You can tour the world
Yes, you can.

Do not look back
Never be discouraged,
Do not be distracted
Cheer on, journey on

Your family would be here
Waiting for your victorious arrival
Son, please do not disappoint.

Christmas Is Here

Welcome dear saviour
Bold and loving man
Gentle, caring and sacrificing
How great thou art!

You are here to save us
A people so unholy
You have come to redeem us
A people so lost and lustful
Welcome, saviour divine.

Come, great redeemer
We appreciate, we appreciate
A call so hard to answer
You took it upon yourself.

Calm and gentle saviour
Tender lamb so holy
Meek and mild, a lover
Welcome, gentle saviour.

Christmas is here
Here for us
For us to be saved
Saved by a kind man
Kind man from above,
Above everything that matters.

Thank you poor saviour

Kind and mild, mild and kind
Redeemer, counselor, protector
Healer, wonderful
Your kingdom we expect
Rule, rule this wicked world.

colophon

Fruits from the Poetry Planet
by Ngozi Olivia Osuoha,
was set with SITKA and HIGHTOWER fonts
by SpiNDec, Treasure Coast, Florida.
The covers were designed
by Kris Haggblom, Port Saint Lucie, Florida.

www.ingramcontent.com/pod-product-compliance
Lightning Source LLC
Chambersburg PA
CBHW030119100526
44591CB00009B/457